OUT LOUD first appeared at the start of 1968, that great year. The collection carries the smell of that year. May its reappearance in 1976 coincide with another, stronger, more clear-eyed 1968 in which the people will take all that is theirs and throw away their chains.

The Annotated
OUT LOUD
by
Adrian Mitchell
"The Naughty Boy of English Letters"
(The Guardian)
"The Frankie Vaughan of Capitalist Verse"
(Sunday Times)

1st edition Cape Goliard 1968
2nd edition CAPE GOLIARD PRESS LTD LONDON 1969.
reprinted by the Writers and Readers'
Publishing Cooperative in 1976
(1st Annotated Edition)

Note: none of the poems in this or any other of my books is to be used for examination purposes.

© Copyright Adrian Mitchell. 1969
Standard Book Number 206.61803.4

© Copyright Adrian Mitchell. 1969
Standard Book Number: 206.61803.4

ISBN 0 904613 33 X

Printed in Great Britain by offset lithography by
Billing & Sons Ltd, Guildford, London and Worcester

in front of us a curious figure was standing, a little crouched, legs straddled, arms out-

Seven Songs from US

(a show directed by Peter Brook for the Royal Shakespeare Company. Its faults were huge but it was one of the first works to break the collaborative silence of the British theatre about that war in Vietnam — despite the initial effort of the Lord Chamberlain to ban the show totally.)

stretched from his sides, he had no eyes and his body, most of which was visible through

tatters of burnt rags, was covered with a hard black crust speckled with yellow pus. . . .

(spoken by someone with power to someone in their power — jailer to prisoner, teacher to pupil, parent to child, husband to wife etc. etc. . . . . .)

ICARUS SHMICARUS

If you never spend your money
you know you'll always have some cash.
If you stay cool and never burn
you'll never turn to ash.
If you lick the boots that kick you
then you'll never feel the lash,
and if you crawl along the ground
at least you'll never crash.
So why why why—
WHAT MADE YOU THINK YOU COULD FLY?

Question: Why can't the victim in the poem fly?
Answer: The person who speaks the poem has cut off the victim's wings.

the interpreter said 'he has to stand, cannot sit or lie.' he had to stand-because his

ZAPPING THE CONG

I'm really rockin' the Delta
From coast to coast.
Got em crawling for shelter,
Got em burning like toast.
And the President told me
It wouldn't take long,
But I'm Zapping the Cong.

Zapping the Cong
Back where they belong.
Hide your yellow asses
When you hear my song.
All over the jungle,
Up to old Haiphong,
Been crapping jelly petrol,
I been zap-zap-zap-zap Zapping the Cong.

Had a bomb in my 'copter
Called Linda B.*
Saw a village and dropped her
On a mess of VC.
But I always say sorry
When I get it wrong.
Then I got to be zooming,
'Cause I'm Zapping the Cong.

Zapping the Cong
Back where they belong.
Hide your yellow asses
When you hear my song.
All over the jungle,
Up to old Haiphong,
Been crapping jelly petrol,
I been zap-zap-zap-zap Zapping the Cong.

*censored by the Lord Chamberlain

dy was no longer covered with a skin but with a crust like crackling which broke easily.

I had a dream about going
With Ho Chi Minh.
But I'll only be crowing
When I'm zapping Pekin.
I'll be spreading my jelly
With a happy song
'Cause I'm screwing all Asia*
When I'm zapping the Cong.

Zapping the Cong
Back where they belong.
Hide your yellow asses
When you hear my song.
All over the jungle,
Up to old Haiphong,
Been crapping jelly petrol,
I been zap-zap-zap-zap Zapping the Cong.

(goes to the tune of <u>Sweet Little Sixteen</u>. based on an amazing article by the late Nick Tomalin — a fine journalist and a wonderful friend. I don't dedicate this one to him, though. There are others he'd prefer. Take your pick, Nick).

*typed as " 'Cause ah's crewing all Asia" — (image of a Southerner acting as cox of a boat rowed by the entire population of Asia) — this line was passed by the Lord Chamberlain.

in front of us a curious figure was standing, a little crouched, legs straddled, arms ou

ANY COMPLAINTS?

My girl Kate's teaching in the States,
Lecturing from town to town.
Pays her bills by, gets her thrills by
Studying the influence of Yeats on Yeats—

(CHORUS)
What's wrong with that?
What's wrong with that?
That's what she always wanted to be.
What's wrong with that?
If it makes her happy,
If it keeps her happy,
That's all that should matter to me.

My son Dave says he's living in a cave,
Hiding from the MI5.
Rank outsider, full of cider,
Goes to demonstrations for a good old rave.

(CHORUS)

My son Pete has a passion for defeat,
Never leaves the Twilight Zone.
He's a chronic melancholic
Chewing tranquilisers while he sits and sits.

(CHORUS)

My son Tom sends chatty letters from
Where they make pneumonic plaque.
Scientific, feels terrific
Breeding germs to go into the Black Death Bomb.

etched from his sides. he had no eyes and his body, most of which was visible through

(CHORUS)

My name's Adrian Mitchell and I like a bit of asymmetry
around the place so that's why verse three, as you'll have
noticed, has a fouled-up rhyme scheme, more fun that
way and—

What's wrong with that?
What's wrong with that?
That's what I always wanted to do.
What's wrong with that?
If it makes me happy,
If it keeps me happy,
That's all that should matter to you.

tatters of burnt rags, was covered with a hard black crust speckled with yellow pus ...

WHEN DREAMS COLLIDE

Red dreams, white dreams,
Dreams of freedom and power.
Driving faster down the highway,
Speeding along at a hundred deaths an hour.
Some think they're driving to Jerusalem
When they're heading for Genocide.
Small dreams, big dreams,
All seem bad dreams—
When dreams collide.

You're sucking your consensus when in walks the White Power Man
And he sells you a dream on the military instalment plan.
It's a supercharged vision and it shines like the Milky Way,
So you sign the agreement 'cause he says you'll never have to pay.

You're driving this Cadillac, your heart feels like the sun.
You're Rockefellersuperchrist, your numberplate just says One.
There's an engine full of gin and a blonde who works by steam
In your souped-up million-carat swinging hell of a dream.

Well the sunset looks like a Colour Supplement spread
And you can't slow down to count the Indonesian dead.
Then the brakes go crazy so you flash all your lights and pray
Because you've seen another dream and it's travelling the other way.

It's a huge red tractor and it's coming on too damn fast
And the road's too narrow and you know that you'll never get past.
But the radio shouts that your dream has got to go through
And the last thing you see is the tractor-driver looks like you.

Red dreams, white dreams,
Dreams of freedom and power,
Driving faster down the highway,
Speeding along at a hundred deaths an hour.
Some think they're driving to Jerusalem
When they're heading for Genocide.
Small dreams, big dreams,
All seem bad dreams—
When dreams collide.

he interpreter said 'he has to stand, cannot sit or lie'. he had to stand-because his

STIMULATING SONG

We know what we're doing.
We know what we're doing it for.
We know what we're doing.
We ought to know
For we've done it before.
We know what we're doing.
We know who we're doing it to.
We know what we're doing.
Out of the way
Or you know what we do.
Out of the way
Or we'll do it to you.

body was no longer covered with a skin but with a crust like crackling which broke easily

MAKE AND BREAK

Pass me the stethoscope of Albert Schweitzer,
Pass me the armoury of Mickey Spillane.
Put the mothers through the bacon-slicer,
Pick up the pieces and fit them together again.

Want to be humane, but we're only human.
Off with the old skin, on with the new.
We maim by night.
We heal by day.
Just the same as you.

Fill all the area with whirling metal,
Five thousand razor-blades are slashing like rain.*
Mr Hyde has a buddy called Jekyll
Picks up the pieces and fits them together again.

Want to be humane, but we're only human.
Off with the old skin, on with the new.
We maim by night.
We heal by day.
Just the same as you.

We treat the enemy like real blood brothers
God made the family a blessing and pain.
Wives and husbands vivisect each other,
Pick up the pieces and fit them together again. †

Want to be humane, but we're only human.
Off with the old skin, on with the new.
We maim by night.
We heal by day.
Just the same as you.

* Lazy Dog
† Of course this argument — that we are all as guilty as the mass-murderers because we are inept and sometimes cruel in our personal relations — is totally specious and this should be clear in any performance.

n front of us a curious figure was standing, a little crouched, legs straddled, arms out-

MOON OVER MINNESOTA
(a true story
to catch the rhythm — think of it as a
double bass solo by, say, Jimmy Blanton)

Mister Bondhus
Of Big Lake,
Minnesota
Made his mistake
When he raised ten sons,
Ten sons, ten sons,
To be Henry Fondas—
You know, the model of a democratic voter—
Didn't buy his sons guns.
Why?
Didn't want them to die
Or kill. Was that strange?
Well yes
I guess
But it makes for a change.
One day the draft board
Told Mister Bondhus
You can afford
To let the Army have a son
Just one
For a start,
You can part
With Barry, Barry,
Barry Barry Bondhus—
Your son.

Mister Bondhus
Of Big Lake,
Minnesota,
Downright
Forthright
Wouldn't send his quota.
Jefferson's sake
I'm not the kind of man who squanders
His seed.

stretched from his sides. he had no eyes and his body, most of which was visible throug

I need
Barry, if you draft him
I've got nothing to
Look forward to
But ten coffins draped with the flag.
It became
A game
Of tag.
Will the draft board
Catch Barry Bondhus
To join the boys who died
On the side
Of the Lord
And the Big Lake
Minnesota
Draft Board?

Barry Bondhus
Of big Lake,
Minnesota,
Ponders
As he wanders
Through the doors of the draft board
Office
Of his
Own accord.
Opens half a dozen files
Packed full,
Stacked full
With miles and miles,
Piles of government documents
About all the young men due to go far.
Then he lumps in,
Dumps in—
If I may quote a

atters of burnt rags, was covered with a hard black crust speckled with yellow pus. . . .

Story from the Minneapolis Star—
Two full buckets of human excrement,
Stinking
Bondhus think-in
Excrement—
Nothing personal against the President—*
It sounds as wild
As the action of a sewer—
realist child,
But the draft board files
Are all defiled.

Walt Whitman
Charlie Parker
Clarence Darrow
Ben Shahn.
William Burroughs
Allen Ginsberg
Woody Guthrie
Tom Paine.
James Baldwin
Joseph Heller
Dr Benjamin Spock
Mark Twain.

Yes all of the beautiful prophets of America
Write across the Minnesota sky:
Look look look at Barry Bondhus—
That boy can fly.

*L.B.J.

the interpreter said 'he has to stand, cannot sit or lie'. he had to stand-because hi

body was no longer covered with a skin but with a crust like crackling which broke easily.

Lyrics, Poems, Word – Cartoons

in front of us a curious figure was standing, a little crouched, legs straddled, arms ou

stretched from his sides. he had no eyes and his body, most of which was visible through

SELF-CONGRATULATING, SELF-DEPRECATING, AUTO-DESTRUCTIVE BLUES
(quick ego-trip to get a load of that stuff out of the way)

If you're betting on the horses, you know you've got to follow form,
Got to vet up on the set-up and get up and bet on form,
I was losing losing losing before I was even born.

You may come from Venezuela, but I was born on Mars,
Venice or Venus or Venezuela, but I was raised on Mars,
I've got a head full of meteorites, heart full of little green children and
    balls full of shooting stars.

So if you want a good investment, better not buy me.
I'm on the edge of the ledge and I'm not gilt-edged so your broker will
    advise I'm a joker so get wise and don't buy me.
Some men are like insurance, but I'm more like—suck it and see.

tatters of burnt rags, was covered with a hard black crust speckled with yellow pus. . . .

TO YOU

I was born in 1932. This poem was written as a note to my wife just before my one and only breakdown. Later I found that many other people had passed through a very similar sequence of experiences and that it was not a private wail but a public poem. Just after the same breakdown I wrote Peace is Milk, which is at the end of this book

One: we were swaddled, ugly-beautiful and drunk on milk.
Two: cuddled in arms always covered by laundered sleeves.
Three: we got sand and water to exercise our imaginative faculties.
Four: we were hit. Suddenly hit.

Five: we were fed to the educational system limited.
Six: worried by the strange creatures in our heads, we strangled some of
    them.
Seven: we graduated in shame.
Eight: World War Two and we hated the Germans as much as our secret
          bodies, loved the Americans as much as the Russians, hated
          killing, loved killing. depending on the language in the Bible
          in the breast pocket of the dead soldier, we were crazy-thirsty
          for Winston Superman, for Jesus with his infinite tommy-gun
          and the holy Spitfires, while the Jap dwarfs hacked through
          the undergrowth of our nightmares—there were pits full of
          people-meat—and the real bombs came, but they didn't hit us,
          my love, they didn't hit us exactly.
My love, they are trying to drive us mad.

So we got to numbers eight, nine, ten, and eleven,
Growing scales over every part of our bodies,
Especially our eyes,
Because scales were being worn, because scales were armour.
And now we stand, past thirty, together, madder than ever,
We make a few diamonds and lose them.
We sell our crap by the ton.
My love, they are trying to drive us mad.

Make love. We must make love
Instead of making money.
You know about rejection? Hit. Suddenly hit.
Want to spend my life building poems in which untamed
People and animals walk around freely, lie down freely
Make love freely
In the deep loving carpets, stars circulating in the ceiling,
Poems like honeymoon planetariums.
But our time is burning.
My love, they are trying to drive us mad.

the interpreter said 'he has to stand, cannot sit or lie'. he had to stand-because his

Peace was all I ever wanted.
It was too expensive.
My love, they are trying to drive us mad.

Half the people I love are shrinking.
My love, they are trying to drive us mad.

Half the people I love are exploding.
My love, they are trying to drive us mad.

I am afraid of going mad.

(TO YOU has been set to music most powerfully by the great Dutch composer Peter Schat. I'm now working with Peter on a circus opera called HOUDINI.)

BIRTHDAY SONG FOR SPIKE HAWKINS, THE UNHOLY GHOST

She rubbed me in the pub
She rubbed me in the pub
She rubbed me in the pub
NO SINGING ALLOWED!

body was no longer covered with a skin but with a crust like crackling which broke easily.

LULLABY FOR WILLIAM BLAKE

>Blakehead, babyhead,
>Your head is full of light.
>You sucked the sun like a gobstopper.
>Blakehead, babyhead,
>High as a satellite on sunflower seeds,
>First man-powered man to fly the Atlantic,
>Inventor of the poem which kills itself,
>The poem which gives birth to itself,
>The human form, jazz, Jerusalem
>And other luminous, luminous galaxies.
>You out-spat your enemies.
>You irradiated your friends.
>Always naked, you shaven, shaking tyger-lamb,
>Moon-man, moon-clown, moon-singer, moon-drinker,
>You never killed anyone.
>Blakehead, babyhead,
>Accept this mug of crude red wine—
>I love you.

(a reviewer called this one "patronising" because it speaks of Blake as a baby. I think that depends on your attitude to babies).

front of us a curious figure was standing, a little crouched, legs straddled, arms out-

THANK YOU DICK GREGORY

*King Lear kept shouting at his Fool:
"These children squeeze, bruise and knot my arteries.
I ache and shake with fatherhood.
Sex can't ache or shake me now
But bawdiness makes my old eyes shine.
So make me jokes that jump, and tumble,
A whole crowd of jokes, a courtful of pretty people jokes
So I can meet each one just once
And then forget, meeting another joke."
But the Fool made a face like an expensive specialist,
He put one hand on the King's pulse, one on his own heart
And said: "Your Majesty, you're dying, man."

Dick Gregory, the funny man, left the glad clapping hands
Of San Francisco, where tigers still survive,
To walk in the dust of Greenwood, Mississippi.
He walked as Gary Cooper used to walk
In Westerns, but Gregory walked blackly, seriously, not
  pretending.
He burned as Brando burns in movies
But the flames behind his eyes were black
And everything his eyes touched scorched.
His jokes crackled in the air,
Gags like Bob Hope's, but these were armed and black.
Liberals realised that they were dwarfs,
Colonels got blisters, and Gregory laughed.

When Dick Gregory reached the South
They told him his two-month son was dead.
I heard that today.
I had to write to say:
Thank you Dick Gregory,
I send as much love as you will take from me,
My blackest and my whitest love.
King Lear is dying of your jokes,
Of your flames, of your tall walking—
Thank you Dick Gregory.

*King Lear = the White Establishment, which at the time this was written wore the face of John F. Kennedy.

stretched from his sides. he had no eyes and his body, most of which was visible throug

SOMETIMES I FEEL LIKE A CHILDLESS MOTHER

My hands shake, my eyelids tremble.
The tigers in my head assemble.

(another average day in the Valley of the Shadow of Death)

OFFICIAL ANNOUNCEMENT

   Her Majesty's Government has noted with regret
That seven unidentified flying objects are zooming towards the earth.
   Her Majesty's Government has noted with regret
That they look like angels except that their skins and their wings are as
raw as afterbirth.
   Her Majesty's Government has noted with regret
That our military computers wrote a billion-word message explaining why
they all chose suicide
   Her Majesty's Government has noted with regret
That here come the angels, and each of the angels has a jar with an
oceanful of plague inside.

   Her Majesty's Government has noted with regret
That the first angel has poured out his jar and that British nationals
and others who have the mark of the beast or have at some time in the
past worshipped the image of the beast are being afflicted with sores
so noisome and grievous that their bodies are flashing like pinball
machines.
   Her Majesty's Government has noted with regret
That the second angel has poured out his jar and that the sea has
become as the blood of a dead man and that everything in the sea is
dying including Her Majesty's submarines.

:ters of burnt rags, was covered with a hard black crust speckled with yellow pus. . . .

        Her Majesty's Government has noted with regret
That the third angel has poured out his jar and that the Thames has
become an enormous and open and pulsing jugular vein.
        Her Majesty's Government has noted with regret
That the fourth angel has poured out his jar and that the heat of the
sun has become amplified but a spokesman for Civil Defence advises
John Bull to stick his head in a sandbag full of ice in order to
postpone or avert the frying of his brain.
        Her Majesty's Government has noted with regret
That the fifth angel has de-jarred and that—it's all gone dark, we
can't see—and all citizens who do not bear an official seal of
redemption are gnawing their tongues in pain.
        Her Majesty's Government has noted with regret
That the sixth angel—Frog Devils! Unclean! Frog-Beast Armageddon!
        Her Majesty's Government has noted with regret
That the seventh angel—IT IS DONE—voices thunder lightnings great
earthquake such as such as was not since men were upon the earth, so
mighty. an earthquake and so great and every island including us every
island is flying away and regretfully the mountains cannot be found
and a great hail is falling with steel rain and fire that is wet.

All of which things, although we understand the provocation under
which heaven is acting and take this opportunity of reaffirming our
unshaken trust in the general principles and policies of heaven, and in the
firm belief that all possible steps have been taken to ensure minimal
civilian casualties and compassionate underkill—
        Her Majesty's Government has noted with regret.

I was raised in the Fear of the Bible

the interpreter said 'he has to stand, cannot sit or lie'. he had to stand-because h

THIS FRIEND

I've got this friend you see and it was the Cuba crisis and the voices were telling him that there was a plot to set the world on fire and so he shook his way round London lurching deliberately into policemen so they took him in and they knocked out his front teeth and all the time they were knocking out his front teeth they were calling him SIR and after he had been in Brixton for a week or maybe more he doesn't remember they decided he was mad.

This friend now carries a certificate which guarantees that he is schizophrenic.

not any more. he killed himself.
he was a good poet, much loved, in pain.
sleep.

ody was no longer covered with a skin but with a crust like crackling which broke easily.

This one was a hit at the Anarchist Ball at the Fulham Town Hall the night after a General Election and was only marred by the strange noises from the green-faced brothers at the back as they sniffed ether from a rag —

POEM ON THE OCCASION OF THE RETURN OF HER MAJESTY THE QUEEN FROM CANADA —

Some love Jesus and some love brandy
Some love Schweitzer or the boys in blue
Some love squeezing that Handy Andy
But I love model airplane glue
    Gloucester Gladiator
    Super-Constellation
    U2 U2 U2
I can see all of Russia from up here

Once upon a time I couldn't leave the ground
My wings were warping and my props were through
No elastic could turn them round
Till I found model airplane glue
    Supermarine Spitfire
    Vickers Viscount
    Junkers Junkie
Come fly with me

Take one sniff and my engines start
Second sniff I'm Bleriot and Bader too
Holds me together when I'm flying apart
So I love model airplane glue
    BOAC
    El-Al
    Sputnik
I am Eagle I am Eagle

Some love a copper and some love a preacher
Some love Hiroshima and Waterloo
Some love the Beatles and some love Nietzche
But I love model airplane glue
    A bit of wire
    A rubber band
    Balsa wood
    That's man
And a man needs glue.

in front of us a curious figure was standing, a little crouched, legs straddled, arms out-

FOR RACHEL: CHRISTMAS 1965, 1966, 1967, 1968, 1969, 1970, 1971, 1972, 1973, 1974, 1975....

Caesar sleeping in his armoured city
Herod shaking like a clockwork toy
and spies are moving into Rama
asking for a baby boy.

> Caesar is the father of Herod
> Herod is the father of us all
> and we'll be obedient, silent little children
> or the moon will drop
> and the sun will fall.

Someone must have warned the wanted mother
she'll be hiding with her family
and soldiers are marching through Rama
silently, obediently.

> Caesar is the father of Herod
> Herod is the father of us all
> and we'll be obedient, silent little children
> or the moon will drop
> and the sun will fall.

Down all the white-washed alleys of Rama
small soft bodies are bayoneted
and Rachel is weeping in Rama
and will not be comforted.

> Caesar is the father of Herod
> Herod is the father of us all
> and we'll be obedient, silent little children
> or the moon will drop
> and the sun will fall.

retched from his sides. he had no eyes and his body, most of which was visible through

    Caesar sleeping in his armoured city
    Herod dreaming in his swansdown bed
    and Rachel is weeping in Rama
    and will not be comforted

        Caesar is the father of Herod
        Herod is the father of us all
        and we'll be obedient, silent little children
        or the moon will drop
        and the sun will fall.

tatters of burnt rags, was covered with a hard black crust speckled with yellow pus. .

NOTHINGMAS DAY

No it wasn't.

It was Nothingmas Eve and all the children in Notown were not tingling with excitement as they lay unawake in their heaps
    D
     o
      w
       n
        s
         t
          a
           r
s their parents were busily not placing the last crackermugs, glimmerslips and sweetlumps on the Nothingmas Tree.
HEY! but what was that invisible trail of chummy sparks or vaulting stars across the sky?
Father Nothingmas—drawn by 18 or 21 rainmaidens—
Father Nothingmas—his sackbut bulging with air—
Father Nothingmas—was not on his way.
(From the streets of the snowless town came the quiet of unsung carols and the merry silence of the steeple bell).
Next morning the children did not fountain out of bed with cries of WHOOPERATION! They picked up their Nothingmas stockings and with traditional quiperamas such as: "Look what I haven't got! It's just what I didn't want!" pulled their stockings on their ordinary legs.
For breakfast they ate breakfast.
After woods they all avoided the Nothingmas Tree, where Daddy, his face failing to beam like a leaky torch, was not distributing gemgames, sodaguns, golly-trolleys, jars of humdrums and packets of slubberated croakers.
Off, off, off went the children to school, soaking each other with no howls of "Merry Nothingmas and a Happy No Year" and not pulping each other with no-balls.
At school Miss Whatnot taught them how to write No Thank You letters.
Home they burrowed for Nothingmas dinner.

e interpreter said 'he has to stand, cannot sit or lie.' he had to stand-because his

    The table was not groaning under all manner of
NO TURKEY
NO SPICED HAM
NO SPROUTS
NO CRANBERRY JELLYSAUCE
NO NOT NOWT.
    There was not one (1) shoot of glee as the Nothingmas Pudding, unlit, was not brought in. Mince pies were not available, nor was there any demand for them.
    Then, as another Nothingmas clobbered to a close, they all haggled off to bed where they slept happily never after.

and that is not the end of the story

body was no longer covered with a skin but with a crust like crackling which broke easi[ly]

AS I WRITE THIS THERE IS A PROCESSION PASSING MY WINDOW

BANG BANG BANG
TARA CHI-TUM TITA

    I am very old
    I have to get up three times in the morning and sleep after lunch

BANG BANG BANG
TARA CHI-TUM TITA

    I am so old
    I am still paying off my danegeld at a poem a month

VOTE VOTE VOTE FOR MR MANDRAKE
(Scream)
HE'S THE MAN TO SEE YOU THROUGH
BANG BANG

    I am extremely old
    I remember when the coastlines on maps were completely different
    I remember when Mars Bars were as big as sliced loaves
BANG BANG BANG
TARA CHI-TUM TITA

    I am so damned old and tired
    With the sex war the class war the race war the war war

BANG BANG BANG

    I can remember nothing but war

front of us a curious figure was standing, a little crouched, legs straddled, arms out-

BALLADE OF BEANS

(written in Iowa City where I lived with my wife and baby in half a tin shed in Finkbine Park)

Nightmare. A silver butcher's truck
Hurtles around my brain and chop
Goes the neck-chopper. Wake. I suck
Pus from my gums, then slowly prop
Bones till they stand upright. I slop
Water which last night rinsed our greens
Over my face. My coiled guts hop—
The sink is clogged with dead beans.

Truth will lie, panting, for a buck.
Philosophy's a lollipop.
Who heeds Religion's biddy cluck
Or cares when Justice goes flip-flop?
So U.N.O.'s a headless mop,
Peace never reached her early teens,
Terror's capsuled in each raindrop—
The sink is clogged with dead beans.

Switzerland's had a lot of luck,
But Cuba slugged a wealthy cop
And Europe stands where lightning struck
Twice lately. Berlin. Will it drop?
Will the earth's ice-protected top
Flip off to show dead submarines?
The world, the grubby old death shop,
The sink is clogged with dead beans.

*Wilson, we're both about to stop.
England tots up as England gleans
The grains of your crapulous crop—
The sink is clogged with dead beans.

*Well, he did stop. So did I. But we both made comebacks. I think this one was written for Lord Home in the first place. It demonstrates easeful mastery of a complex form, don't it? I know another one about beans:

Beans, beans, the musical fruit
The more you eat the more you toot
The more you toot the better you feel
So I take beans for every meal.

I learnt that one at Oxford. "The musical fruit" is a good phrase. Could be Keats.

THE LIBERAL CHRIST GIVES AN INTERVIEW

I would have walked on the water
But I wasn't fully insured.
And the BMA sent a writ my way
With the very first leper I cured.

I would've preached a golden sermon
But I didn't like the look of the Mount.
And I would've fed fifty thousand
But the Press wasn't there to count.

And the businessmen in the temple
Had a team of ~~coppers~~ heavies on the door.
And if I'd spent a year in the desert
I'd have lost my pension for sure.

I would've turned the water into wine
But they weren't giving licenses.
And I would have died and been crucified
But like—you know how it is.

I'm going to shave off my beard
And cut my hair,
Buy myself some bulletproof
Underwear
I'm the Liberal Christ
And I've got no blood to spare.

tatters of burnt rags, was covered with a hard black crust speckled with yellow pus. . . .

> FOOTNOTES ON CELIA CELIA
> Used to slouch along High Holborn / in my gruesome solo lunch-hours. / It was entirely lined / with Gothick insurance offices / except for one oblong block of a shop / called Gamages, / where, once / drunk, on Christmas Eve, / I bought myself a battery-operated Japanese pig / with a chef's hat on top of his head / and a metal stove which lit up red / and the pig moved a frying pan up and down with his hand / and tossed a plastic fried egg into the air / and caught it again / and then tossed it and caught it again the other way up / and again / all the time emitting squeals of excitement through / a series of holes in the top of his head — but apart from that ... I want to forget High Holborn

CELIA CELIA

When I am sad and weary,
When I think all hope has gone,
When I walk along High Holborn
I think of you with nothing on.

A MACHINE THAT MAKES LOVE AND POEMS AND MISTAKES

> (touch of ego-worry going on here)

The whirring stops, the door in my chest
Slides open. Fatty squeezes out
Smiling like silver. An airliner staircase
Appears under his first step. He podges down
Applauding himself with padded palms.

Next Jagged, wearing his frayed-wire suit,
Scales my legs, jerks through the door and pulls
My starting handle. Thought-gears grind.
He's muddled, pressing all my buttons
Too hard. Not hard enough. His blood is caffeine.

He exits limping, gladly. Then he flops
Prone on the tarmac, hiding his splintered eyes.
His place is taken. This one's a prodigy,
A milk-faced boy of five who sings to himself
As he tries to play tunes with knobs and levers.

I've got other mechanics. Sometimes they fight
Over my delicate controls. They strike,
Or try to make me fly. They blow my fuses.
Just now I didn't answer. You caught me between shifts.
Ask again now. Someone will answer you.

the interpreter said 'he has to stand, cannot sit or lie.' he had to stand-because his

(the Flower Power craze prompted this title, blossom.)

TAKE STALK BETWEEN TEETH PULL STALK FROM BLOSSOM THROW BLOSSOM OVERARM TOWARDS ENEMY LIE FLAT AND AWAIT EXPLOSION *AND STILL WAITING*

I staggered in the garage and handed them my heart.
"Can you overhaul it cos the bloody thing won't start?"
They hammered it and sprayed it till it looked just like a toad,
They told me that it shouldn't be allowed on the road.
They said I'd better trade it for a psych-e-del-ic screen.
They said "What d'you call this aboriginal machine?"
I said
It's a rose I suppose.

A unicorn is bathing in the shallows of your eyes.
You've got a mouth that's whispering between your thighs
You bring me foreign honeycombs and science fiction ties
And every time you touch me you declare your surprise.
Your language is a code that I haven't yet cracked
So I can't be sure of your message for a fact
But
It's a rose I suppose.

When they see us walking, they're puzzled what to say.
We're so obvious in a mysterious way—
Clouds that fly south when the wind goes east,
Hovercraft feet and faces all creased
We draw our wages in musical wine
And what our business is, well that's harder to define
But
It's a rose I suppose.

Well Tennyson's on television selling bad breath.
~~Lyndon's in the pulpit and the sermon is death~~
Hitler's in the bunker playing nuclear chess,
Judas got a column on the Sunday Express.
The zombies are lurching all over the town,
There's only one weapon that seems to bring them down
And
It's a rose I suppose.

kissinger's the preacher and the sermon's still death.

body was no longer covered with a skin but with a crust like crackling which broke easily.

THE PRINCE OF WAILERS

Edward the Eighth
crazy king
He knew how to shake that thing.

(see "Crown Matrimonial" by Royce Ryton which deals with the Abdication Crisis and is one of the funniest plays ever written)

BRIEFING

He may be fanatical, he may have a madness.
Either way, move carefully.
He must be surrounded, but he's contagious.

One of you will befriend his family.
One male and one female will love the subject
Until he loves you back. Gradually

Our team will abstract and collect
His mail, nail-clippings, garbage, friends, words, schemes,
Graphs of his fears, scars, sex and intellect.

Steam open his heart. Tap his dreams.
Learn him inside and inside out.
When he laughs, laugh. Scream when he screams.

He will scream. "Innocent!" He'll shout
Until his mouth is broken with stones.
We use stones. We take him out

in front of us a curious figure was standing, a little crouched, legs straddled, arms out-

To a valley full of stones.
He stands against a shed. He stands on stones
Naked. The initial stones

Shower the iron shed. Those stones
Outline the subject. When he cries for stones
The clanging ceases. Then we give him stones,

Filling his universe with stones.
Stones—his atoms turn to stones
And he becomes a stone buried in stones.

A final tip. Then you may go.
Note the half-hearted stoners and watch how
Your own arm throws. And watch how I throw.

etched from his sides. he had no eyes and his body, most of which was visible through

THE SUN LIKES ME
*"The sun likes me"—Spanish way of saying "I like the sun"—
they are a proud people*

      The sun likes me.
Maybe I've been lying out in the Mayakovsky too long.
Maybe my mind's been a breast-stroke commuter between London and New York too long.
Maybe I've been longing too long.

      The sun likes me.
Maybe it's because my dynamic tension comic-strip bible hath taught me
      that it's better to kick sand into the sunlight and watch how it
      shimmers than kick it in a twenty-stone muscleman's face.
And maybe it's because my atoms won't stand still because they want to
      rock and roll all over the place—

But she taught me to say it.
I was near enough to lick her
And I licked her like the sun licks me and
WOW
She was a buxom anchovy.
Through both our sunrise sunset bodies I heard her say:
"Repeat it after me—
The sun likes me."
So I said it (and I believe it):
      The sun likes me.

I woke up full of business.
After a two-day year at the Registry of Companies I discovered that a 61
      per majority on the board of the sun was held by a holding
      company (Sol Investments) represented by Phoebus Nominees
      who were nominated by a legalistic fabrication called Icarus
      Consolidation half-immersed in liquidation.
And the only stockholder—
Thanks to Auntie Irma's will—
The only stockholder
Was ME.

tatters of burnt rags, was covered with a hard black crust speckled with yellow pus. .

>	I seem to have changed.
>		The sun likes me.
>	I'm indifferent.
>		The sun doesn't like me.
>	See if I care.
>		For like it or lump it,
>	I own it.

Last week I found I'd left my Barclaycard in Das Kapital but when the bill came round I simply reached into my asbestos wallet, produced the aforesaid golden disc or orb and you should have seen the faces of the waiters or their feet for that matter as they blushed to the colour of burnt semolina—

>	Because I own the sun,
>	The only one.
>	Mine, mine,
>	Sixty-one per cent of it,
>		MINE.

(Copyright of this poem belongs to SUNPOEM EXPLOITATION INC. a branch of Unilever — motto — "Give me somewhere to stand and with this Unilever I will move the Earth")

interpreter said 'he has to stand, cannot sit or lie.' he had to stand-because his

LOVE FOR TONY

      Tony Jackson is a walking jungle.
      Tony Jackson can cry.
      Tony Jackson, when elected, will encourage breasts.
      Tony Jackson will lend you his invisible roller-skates.
      Tony Jackson bawls back at you, balls back at you.
      Tony Jackson sweats the blues.
      Tony Jackson can't give you anything but love, baby.
      Tony Jackson is alight.
      Tony Jackson, when elected, will encourage jungle.
      Tony Jackson is a walking ball.
      Tony Jackson can't give you anything but blue sweat, baby.
      Tony Jackson will lend you breasts.
      Tony Jackson sweats roller-skates.
      Tony Jackson, when elected, will cry.

body was no longer covered with a skin but with a crust like crackling which broke easil

FROM RICH UNEASY AMERICA TO MY FRIEND CHRISTOPHER LOGUE
"Never again that sick feeling when the toilet overflows"
advertisement: *The Iowa City Press-Citizen.*

    Jim Hall's guitar walking around
    As if the Half Note's wooden floor
    Grew blue flowers and each flower
    Drank from affluent meadow ground.
    The lush in the corner dropped his sorrowing
    When he noticed his hands and elbows dancing.
    Long silver trucks made lightning past the window.
    A two-foot hunter watch hung from the ceiling.
    Then you prowled in. The guitar splintered,
    The lush held hands with himself, trucks concertinaed.
    The watch-hands shook between Too Late and Now.

    As I sit easy in the centre
    Of the U.S. of America,
    Seduced by cheeseburgers, feeling strong
    When bourbon licks my lips and tongue,
    Ears stopped with jazz or both my eyes
    Full of Mid-Western butterflies,
    You drive out of a supermarket
    With petrol bombs in a family packet
    And broadcast down your sickened nose:
    "It overflows. By Christ, it overflows."

n front of us a curious figure was standing, a little crouched, legs straddled, arms out-

I TRIED, I REALLY TRIED

    Mesh-faced loudspeakers outshouted Fleet Street,
    Their echoes overlapping down Shoe Lane
    And Bouverie Street, pronouncing:
    WASH YOURSELF POET.
    Blurred black police cars from the BBC
    Circled me blaring: WASH YOURSELF POET
    AND DON'T FORGET YOUR NAVEL.
    My ears were clogged with savoury gold wax
    And so I failed WASH to hear at first WASH
    WASH WASH YOURSELF
    Since I was naked and they wore
    Chrome-armoured cars and under the cars man-made fibre
        suits and under the suits Y-front pants and under the
        pants official groin protectors and under the groin
        protectors automatics,
    I obediently ran to the city's pride,
    The Thames, that Lord Mayor's Procession of mercury,
    And jumped from Westminster Bridge.
    Among half-human mud I bathed
    Using a dead cat for a loofah,
    Detergent foam for gargle.
    I dived, heard the power station's rumble and the moan of
        sewers.
    The bubbles of my breath exploded along the waterskin.
    Helmeted in dead newspapers, I sprang
    Into the petrol-flavoured air
    And Big Ben, like a speak-your-weight machine
    Intoned WATCH YOURSELF POET.
    Clothed in the muck of London, I yelled back:
    I HAVE BEEN WASHED IN THE BLOOD OF THE
        THAMES, BIG BROTHER,
    AND FROM NOW ON I SHALL USE NO OTHER.

1. Oxford Mail. Reporter. Left and went to —
2. Evening Standard. Diary reporter and reporter. Left for the
3. Daily Mail. Pop record columnist. Quit for —
4. The Sun. TV critic. Left that for —
5. The Sunday Times. TV critic. Sacked.
6. Peace News and The Black Dwarf.

stretched from his sides. he had no eyes and his body, most of which was visible through

IT'S A CLEAN MACHINE
(*To the Beatles and Albert Hunt*)

A cop needs a gangster, gangsters need cops,
Fire against fire and it never stops,
But I don't want a fire, I've got underskin heating
Thank you.

They know what we're afraid of:
Soundproof cellars, rhinoceros hide,
Genital electrodes, kneecap sledghammers,
The moment when they take off your shoes—
All of the commonplace terrors.
But I won't name my own special fears,
Thank you.

I have been a one-man band to the galaxies over Bradford
As I skated over the rust-coloured pavements singing:
    Ten cents a dance, that's what they pay me
    A four-legged friend, a four-legged friend, he'll never
       let you down.
    Oh you can knock me down, stamp on my face, slander
       my name all over the place
    But we'll meet again, don't know where, don't know
       when—
    There is a laughing policeman, lives along our street,
    You can hear him laughing, when he's on the beat—
    Oh R, I say R-A,
    R-A-T, R-A-T-T,
    R-A-T-T-F, R-A-T-T-F-I-N-K,
    Rattfink (brawawa) Rattfink (brawawa),
    Mona Lisa Mona Lisa men have named you
    So squeeze my lemon baby till the juice runs down my
       leg—
Singing dangerously
As I bulged with the dynamite sticks of love.
They never caught me yet, but they keep trying.

atters of burnt rags, was covered with a hard black crust speckled with yellow pus. . . .

It happens every day.
I'm standing down the lavatory end
Of a shadow-inhabited bar
When in walks the winter gangster-cop
And everyone he passes is gripped by his metal hand
And they wince as the grip tightens
And their faces sag as the grip relaxes.

The loudspeaker says:
An invitation to the glittering world of Robert Farnon—
Then he acts.
His icicles focus on my eyes.
Capone or Fabian, he yawns.
His iced knees, like car bumpers,
Persuade me to the glittering pavement
Where his wide-shouldered Mercedes waits to eat me.
So far, so bad.

But they never warned him at headquarters,
They never told him the end of the story,
They never told him the way it always ends.

For here they come, sudden surrounders,
All of them laughing, all around us,
The gentle, fire-fighting cavalry,
House-high on ladders, crouched to hydrants,
Flashing their scarlet down the boulevard,
Hoses jumping with the pressure of water from
A thousand Welsh waterfalls, a hundred thousand lochs,
Aiming their polished, jerking nozzles—

And here I wish I could record all of their names but they know who they are, the men and women and children I love and those who love me and may the two lists always coincide—

the interpreter said 'he has to stand, cannot sit or lie.' he had to stand-because hi

      All my friends, crimson, helmeted, hatchet-holstered.
      Their hoses slosh him down slush-flushing gutters and:
      "I'm sorry Adrian, I'm sorry," he drizzles,
      "I didn't know you were a member of the Fire Brigade."

body was no longer covered with a skin but with a crust like crackling which broke easily.

NORMAN MORRISON

On November 2nd 1965
in the multi-coloured multi-minded
United beautiful States of terrible America
Norman Morrison set himself on fire
outside the Pentagon.
He was thirty-one, he was a Quaker,
and his wife (seen weeping in the newsreels)
and his three children
survive him as best they can.
He did it in Washington where everyone could see
because
people were being set on fire
in the dark corners of Vietnam where nobody could see.
Their names, ages, beliefs and loves
are not recorded.
This is what Norman Morrison did.
He poured petrol over himself.
He burned.   He suffered.
He died.
That is what he did
in the white heart of Washington
where everyone could see.
He simply burned away his clothes,
his passport, his pink-tinted skin,
put on a new skin of flame
and became
Vietnamese.

Note: Morrison's name and face are known throughout Vietnam because his message was received there with amazement by people who could hardly believe that an American could care that much. The saddest thing was that other people followed "his example". But it wasn't an example, it was an isolated, important statement. Once made it needed no amplification. He said it for all of us.

in front of us a curious figure was standing, a little crouched, legs straddled, arms out

THE ANGELS IN OUR HEADS

Our angels, spiralling,
Climb the sky like two, like one,
With wings flowing and easy-going
Rippling the current of the sun.

Altitude one hundred miles.
Our angels level out and hover,
Humming delirious pop songs,
Quivering at each other.

Silent suddenly, they shrug
Their rainbow wings around each other.
A thousand multi-coloured hairs
Vibrate along each feather.

And then they drop.
Birds in crowds
Watch and admire from
Grandstand clouds.

The angels both spreadeagle, braking,
Over the ocean, gold and deep.
They slide into its heated waters
To sing in bubbles in their sleep.

Waking, they wander underwater,
Gulping the seasoned sea food, free,
Then they take off in fifty yards
Sprinting across the surface of the sea,

Circling waterbirds, circling higher,
Those weighty feathers dry, and then
Zoom up to a hundred miles
And—there they go again.

retched from his sides. he had no eyes and his body, most of which was visible through

> But when they look out through our eyes
> To see the rain piercing like wire
> Or the white wind throw hurtful snow
> Burying men in drifts of pain and fire
>
> Sometimes our angels hunch and huddle,
> Grounded, sad ducks stuck.
> But they should moult and stomp outside,
> Socialists fighting dirty luck.
>
> For they can talk or march against the winter,
> Get home in time for aerobatics, try
> To teach their children to be flyers and swimmers
> In a warm planet with a cleaner sky.

A WARNING
if you keep two angels in a cage
they will eat each other to death

tatters of burnt rags, was covered with a hard black crust speckled with yellow pus...

BIRTHDAYS
(For Ray Charles)

You shout that you're drowning,
You give it everything.
A manager walks by and says:
"That little cat can sing".
You go to bed mad
And you think that's bad
But what you going to do
When you wake up mad?
There'll be no more birthdays.

I'm talking about
Pain man and fear man and shock man and death man,
Not the Hollywood kind.
I'm talking about
Man made of bone made of wood made of stone
By some Frankenstein.
Talking about
Pain man and fear man and shock man and death man,
The crumbling mind.

There was this astronaut
And one day he found
He couldn't talk
Any more to the ground.
The instruments said
He was stuck for eighty years,
His helmet began
To fill up with tears—
And it was his BIRTHDAY.

I'm talking about
Pain man and fear man and shock man and death man,
Not the Hollywood kind.
I'm talking about
Man made of bone made of wood made of stone
By some Frankenstein.
Talking about
Pain man and fear man and shock man and death man
The crumbling mind.

he interpreter said 'he has to stand, cannot sit or lie.' he had to stand-because his

THE ONLY ELECTRICAL CRYSTAL BALL I EVER SAW FLICKERING BEHIND A BAR

What colour?
O the colour of an apple in love,
A tomfool tomato,
Changing its soft electric moods each second—
Intimate maps, galactic anatomical charts
Never to be repeated.
Well one moment it exploded with every brand of crimson,
The next it was awash with the blue of peace—
Ocean, pacific ocean—
Or became a green place swarmed over by dark canals.

I said to the man behind the bar:
Where does it come from?
He said: I made it myself.
I was so glad I laughed.
I said: Where is it going to?
He laughed.

Sunset over Venus in a goldfish bowl.
Silent jukebox with no money-slot
But pulsing with molten rainbows.
Belisha beacon drunkenly standing,
Head back, mouth open,
Under a hundred-foot-high colourfall
Of brandy soda creme de menthe
Sherry-spiked wine of the country
(Plus a secret formula)
Flowing from a vat with a fuller draught
Than the Tuscarora Deep.

This is no magic melon to solve all our dandruff
But a small machine for giving.
It added some light to my happiness.
It is a good planet.
I call it the earth.

body was no longer covered with a skin but with a crust like crackling which broke easily.

LIFE ON THE OVERKILL ESCALATOR

Dogs must be carried because they do not understand.
You examine the shoulders of the man ahead without understanding.

You pass foreign-faced women. They pass you.
They are cardboard, behind glass. They wear lead corsets anyway.

The vibration becomes part of you
Or you become part of the vibration.

The penalty for stopping the escalator is five pounds.
Five pounds is a lot of money.

TO THE STATUES IN POETS' CORNER, WEST— MINISTER ABBEY

(inspired by the decision to admit the dust of Byron to the Abbey)

You stony bunch of pockskinned whiteys,
Why kip in here? Who sentenced you?
They are buying postcards of you,
The girls in safety knickers.
Tombfaces, glumbums,
Wine should be jumping out of all your holes,
You should have eyes that roll, arms that knock things over,
Legs that falter and working cocks.
Listen.
On William Blake's birthday we're going to free you,
Blast you off your platforms with a blowtorch full of brandy
And then we'll all stomp over to the Houses of Parliament
And drive them into the Thames with our bananas.

in front of us a curious figure was standing, a little crouched, legs straddled, arms out-

BANANA

(footnote to previous poem, written after student at a Teachers' Training College asked me to explain "the Banana Symbolism" in my poems.)

a phallus going round a corner

                                              carefully

WHITMAN ON WHEELS

24

Fanfare: in transports over transport
I salute all passenger-carrying machines—
The admirable automobile, the glottal motor-cycle,
The womby capsule bound for Mars,
The tube train, (see how well it fits its tube),
The vibrant diesel, the little engine that could
And all manner of airplanes whether they carry
Hostesses, hogs or horror.
Gargantuan traction engines,
Curmudgeonly diggers, bull-dozers, dinosauric tank-tracked
    cranes,
Zoomers, splutterers, purrers and gliders
I salute you all,
And also the reliable tricycle.

stretched from his sides. he had no eyes and his body, most of which was visible through

TO NYE BEVAN DESPITE HIS CHANGE OF HEART

Because I loved him
I believe that somebody dropped blood-freezing powder
Into the water-jug of vodka which Nye Bevan swigged
Before he asked us:
Do you want Britain to go naked to the conference table?

A difficult question.
Whoever saw Britain naked?
Britain bathes behind locked doors
Where even the loofah is subject to the Official Secrets Act.
But surely Britain strips for love-making?
Not necessarily.
An analysis of British sexual response
Proves that most of the United Kingdom's acts of love
Have been undertaken unilaterally.
There have been persistently malicious rumours
From Africa and Asia
That Britain's a habitual rapist
But none of the accusers have alleged
That Britain wore anything less than full dress uniform
With a jangle of medals, bash, bash,
During the alleged violations.

So do you want Britain to go naked to the conference table?
Britain the mixed infant,
Its mouth sullen as it enters its second millenium
Of pot-training.
Britain driven mad by puberty,
Still wearing the uniform of Lord Baden-Powell
(Who was honoured for his services to sexual mania).
Britain laying muffins at the Cenotaph.
Britain, my native archipelago
Entirely constructed of rice pudding.

atters of burnt rags, was covered with a hard black crust speckled with yellow pus. . . .

So do you want Britain to go naked to the conference table?
Yes. Yes Nye, without any clothes at all.
For underneath the welded Carnaby
Spike-studded dogcollar groincrusher boots,
Blood-coloured combinations
And the golfing socks which stink of Suez,
Underneath the Rolls Royce heart
Worn on a sleeve encrusted with royal snot,
Underneath the military straitjacket
From the Dead Meat Boutique—
    Lives
    A body
Of incredibly green beauty.

the interpreter said 'he has to stand, cannot sit or lie.' he has to stand—because h

JOHN KEATS EATS HIS PORRIDGE *

It was hot enough to blister
the red paint of his mouth.
But if he let it lie there, glistening,
then clipped segments from the circumference,
it slid down like a soggy bobsleigh.

Grey as November, united as the kingdom,
but the longer he stared into that disc of porridge
the more clearly he traced
under the molten sugar
the outline of each flake of oatmeal.

When the milk made its slow blue-tinted leap from jug to
    bowl
the porridge became an island.
John's spoon vibrated in his hand.
The island became a planet.
He made continents, he made seas.

This is strange porridge.
Eat it all up.

* I regard porridge as a toy rather than a food. An educational toy, mind.

dy was no longer covered with a skin but with a crust like crackling which broke easily.

SUNDAY POEM
(To the Christians)

Eat this: God has a place,
Incense-deodorized, a vaulted mouth
Where the good dead always
Alleluia among towers of teeth.
Boring? In that honey of saliva?
They tell me male sharks come for seven
Or eight hours. Multiply forever—
You still can't count the heaven of Heaven.

Eat this: God has another place,
A gaol-hole. Walls contract and crush
Necks onto legs, bellies into faces
And all parts in a constipated hash
Of cancered madmen, vomiting and skinned,
Skewered in flames which rot, restore and rot,
Breathing only the tear-gas of their sins—
That's what the bad dead get.

in front of us a curious figure was standing, a little crouched, legs straddled, arms out

ALL NIGHT LONG

    SUNDREAM
        SUNSLEEP
    NIGHTBREAK   you
        MOONFLOW   are
    STARFLIGHT   asleep
        MOONSET   beside
    LIGHTGATHER   me
        DAYFALL

[handwritten note: JUST AN EXTRA POEM]

How many narrow strips of hide
Are woven in those sandal shoes?
One hundred and sixty-seven —
Robinson Crusoe knows

retched from his sides. he had no eyes and his body, most of which was visible through

C'MON EVERYBODY
(dedicated to Chubby Checker who introduced the people of Britain to the concept of the pelvis)

There's a grand old dance that's rockin the nation
Shake your money and shut your mouth
Takin the place of copulation
S'called The Bourgeois.

See that girl with the diamond thing?
Shake your money and shut your mouth
Didn't get that by ~~canvassing~~ picketing
She done The Bourgeois.

Do-gooder, do-gooder where you been?
Shake your money and shut your mouth
Done myself good, got a medal from the Queen
For The Bourgeois.

    Is it a singer? No.
    Is it a lover? No.
    Is it a bourgeois? Yeaaah!

Wave your missile around the vault
Shake your money and shut your mouth
Somebody suffers well it ain't your fault
That you're Bourgeois.

I play golf so I exist
Shake your money and shut your mouth
Eye on the ball and hand over fist
I do The Bourgeois.

Five days a week on the nine-eleven
Shake your money and shut your mouth
When we die we'll go to Bournemouth
Cos we're Bourgeois.

tatters of burnt rags, was covered with a hard black crust speckled with yellow pus...

YOU GET USED TO IT
"Am I in Alabama or am I in hell?" A minister, Montgomery, Alabama, March 1965

Begging-bowl eyes, begging-bowl eyes,
skin round hoops of wire.
They do not eat, they are being eaten,
saw them in the papers.

> But it's only bad if you know it's bad,
> fish don't want the sky.
> If you've spent all your life in hell or Alabama
> you get used to it.

Ignorant husband, ignorant wife,
each afraid of the other one's bomb.
He spends all he has in the Gentlemen's
on a half-crown [50p] book of nudes.

> But it's only bad if you know it's bad,
> fish don't want the sky.
> If you've spent all your life in hell or Alabama
> you get used to it.

Beautiful blossom of napalm
sprouting from the jungle,
bloom full of shrivelling things,
might be mosquitoes, might be men.

> But it's only bad if you know it's bad,
> fish don't want the sky.
> If you've spent all your life in hell or Alabama
> you get used to it.

I hurt, you hurt, he hurts, she hurts,
we hurt, you hurt, they hurt.
What can't be cured must go to jail,
what can't be jailed must die.

> But it's only bad if you know it's bad,
> fish don't want the sky.
> If you've spent all your life in hell or Alabama
> you get used to it.

he interpreter said 'he has to stand, cannot sit or lie.' he had to stand-because his

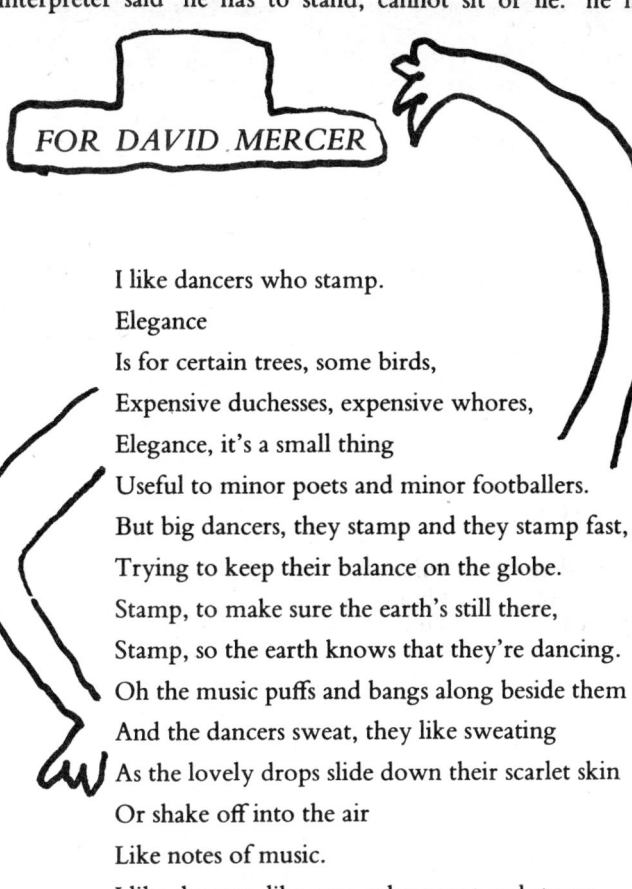

FOR DAVID MERCER

I like dancers who stamp.
Elegance
Is for certain trees, some birds,
Expensive duchesses, expensive whores,
Elegance, it's a small thing
Useful to minor poets and minor footballers.
But big dancers, they stamp and they stamp fast,
Trying to keep their balance on the globe.
Stamp, to make sure the earth's still there,
Stamp, so the earth knows that they're dancing.
Oh the music puffs and bangs along beside them
And the dancers sweat, they like sweating
As the lovely drops slide down their scarlet skin
Or shake off into the air
Like notes of music.
I like dancers, like you, who sweat and stamp
And crack the ceiling when they jump.

body was no longer covered with a skin but with a crust like crackling which broke easi[...]

I AM BOJ
(To be shouted at children who wake early)

I am Boj
I crackle like the Wig of a Judge
I am Boj

I am Boj
My eyes boil over with Hodge-Podge
I am Boj

I am Boj
Organised Sludge and a Thunder-Wedge
I am Boj

I am Boj
I am a Tower of solid Grudge
I am Boj

I am Boj
The molten Centre, the cutting Edge
I am Boj

I am Boj
From blackest Dudgeon I swing my Bludgeon
I am Boj

U–S–S–R SPELLS HAPPY

(sing the first three lines rowdily to the tune of "What Shall We Do With the Drunken Sailor?")

JOLLY OLD, JOLLY OLD DOSTOEVSKY,
JOLLY OLD, JOLLY OLD DOSTOEVSKY,
JOLLY OLD, JOLLY OLD DOSTOEVSKY,
HE WENT TO THE TALKIES
with the Gorkies.

front of us a curious figure was standing, a little crouched, legs straddled, arms out-

HEAR THE VOICE OF THE CRITIC

There are too many colours.
The Union Jack's all right, selective,
Two basic colours and one negative,
Reasonable, avoids confusion.
   (Of course I respect the red, white and blue)

But there are too many colours.
The rainbow, well it's gaudy, but I am
Bound to admit, a useful diagram
When treated as an optical illusion.
   (Now I'm not saying anything against rainbows)

But there are too many colours.
Take the sea. Unclassifiable.
The sky—the worst offender of all,
Tasteless as Shakespeare, especially at sunset.
   (I wish my body were all one colour).

There are too many colours.
I collect flat white plates.
You ought to see my flat white plates.
In my flat white flat I have a perfect set,
   (It takes up seven rooms).

There are too many colours.

stretched from his sides. he had no eyes and his body, most of which was visible throug

MIDNIGHT MARY FROM LLANDUDNO

Midnight Mary from Llandudno
stomped in the bar and ordered vinegar and water,
vinegar and water.

She beat out her heartbeat on the photo of a baby—
My husband was the root of all evil.
I want vinegar and water.

She rocked from her thighs, rocked from her hips
and she slapped out the rhythm with her flat old feet
but they wouldn't give her any vinegar and water.

Well, thank you for the vinegar and water.
Thank you for the vinegar and water.
Thank you for the vinegar and water.

SLAM

tters of burnt rags, was covered with a hard black crust speckled with yellow pus. . . .

LEAFLETS [*]
(For Brian Patten and my twelve students at Bradford)

Outside the plasma supermarket
I stretch out my arm to the shoppers and say:
"Can I give you one of these?"

I give each of them a leaf from a tree.

The first shopper thanks me.
The second puts the leaf in his mack pocket where his wife won't see.
The third says she is not interested in leaves. She looks like a mutilated willow.
The fourth says: "Is it art?" I say that it is a leaf.
The fifth looks through his leaf and smiles at the light beyond.
The sixth hurls down his leaf and stamps it till dark purple mud oozes through.
The seventh says she will press it in her album.
The eighth complains that it is an oak leaf and says he would be on my side if I were also handing out birch leaves, apple leaves, privet leaves and larch leaves. I say that it is a leaf.
The ninth takes the leaf carefully and then, with a backhand fling, gives it its freedom.
It glides, following surprise curving alleys through the air.
It lands. I pick it up.
The tenth reads both sides of the leaf twice and then says: "Yes, but it doesn't say who we should kill."

But you took your leaf like a kiss.

They tell me that, on Saturdays,
You can be seen in your own city centre
Giving away forests, orchards, jungles.

* *two girls went and did this poem[†] with such success that they are both now stars in the "Talkies"!*

† *in the street.*

the interpreter said 'he has to stand, cannot sit or lie.' he had to stand-because h

ADRIAN MITCHELL'S FAMOUS WEAK BLADDER BLUES

Now some praise God because he gave us the bomb to drop in 1945
But I thank the Lord for equipping me with the fastest cock alive.

You may think a sten-gun's frequent, you can call greased lightning fast,
But race them down to the Piccadilly bog and watch me zooming past.

    Well it's excuse me,
    And I'll be back.
    Door locked so rat-a-tat-tat.
    You mind if I go first?
    I'm holding this cloudburst.
    I'll be out in 3.7 seconds flat.

I've got the *Adamant Trophy, the *Niagara Cup, you should see me on the
    M.1 run,
For at every comfort station I've got a reputation for—doing the ton.

Once I met that Speedy Gonzales and he was first through the door.
But I was unzipped, let rip, zipped again and out before he could even draw.

Now God killed ~~Vicky~~ [Lenny Bruce] and he let ~~Harold Wilson~~ [Bob Hope] survive,
But the good Lord blessed little Adrian Mitchell with the fastest cock alive.

* lavatory trademarks

body was no longer covered with a skin but with a crust like crackling which broke easily.

TO WHOM IT MAY CONCERN
(not about the Vietnam War but about being in Britain during that war).

I was run over by the truth one day.
Ever since the accident I've walked this way
    So stick my legs in plaster
    Tell me lies about Vietnam.

Heard the alarm clock screaming with pain,
Couldn't find myself so I went back to sleep again
    So fill my ears with silver
    Stick my legs in plaster
    Tell me lies about Vietnam.

Every time I shut my eyes all I see is flames.
Made a marble phone book and I carved all the names
    So coat my eyes with butter
    Fill my ears with silver
    Stick my legs in plaster
    Tell me lies about Vietnam.

I smell something burning, hope it's just my brains.
They're only dropping peppermints and daisy-chains
    So stuff my nose with garlic
    Coat my eyes with butter
    Fill my ears with silver
    Stick my legs in plaster
    Tell me lies about Vietnam.

Where were you at the time of the crime?
Down by the Cenotaph drinking slime
    So chain my tongue with whisky
    Stuff my nose with garlic
    Coat my eyes with butter
    Fill my ears with silver
    Stick my legs in plaster
    Tell me lies about Vietnam.

in front of us a curious figure was standing, a little crouched, legs straddled, arms out-

> You put your bombers in, you put your conscience out,
> You take the human being and you twist it all about
>   So scrub my skin with women
>   Chain my tongue with whisky
>   Stuff my nose with garlic
>   Coat my eyes with butter
>   Fill my ears with silver
>   Stick my legs in plaster
>   Tell me lies about Vietnam.

A GOOD IDEA

It should be the kind which stiffens and grows a skin
But the creamier kind will do.
Anyway, the Royal Albert Hall must be filled with custard.

stretched from his sides. he had no eyes and his body, most of which was visible through

PEACE IS MILK

Peace is milk.
War is acid. *
The elephant dreams of bathing in lakes of milk.
Acid blood
Beats through the veins
Of the monstrous, vulture-weight fly,
Shaking, rocking his framework.

The elephants, their gentle thinking shredded
By drugs disseminated in the electricity supply,
Sell their children, buy tickets for the Zoo
And form a dead-eyed queue
Which stretches from the decorative, spiked gates
To the enormous shed where the flies are perching.

Peace is milk
War is acid.
Sometimes an elephant finds a bucket of milk.
Swash! and it's empty.
The fly feeds continually.
The fly bulges with acid
Or he needs more. And more.

An overweight fly levers himself
From his revolving chair,
Paces across the elephantskin floor,
Presses a button
And orders steak, steak, elephant steak
And a pint of acid.

Peace is milk.
War is acid.
The elephants are being dried in the sun.
The huge flies overflow.

*the acid in the poem has nothing to do with LSD, but the NBG TLS thought it did.

tatters of burnt rags, was covered with a hard black crust speckled with yellow pus. . . .

Look down from the plane.
Those clouds of marvellous milk.
Easily they swing by on the wind,
Assembling, disassembling,
Forming themselves into pleasure-towers,
Unicorns, waterfalls, funny faces;
Swimming, basking, dissolving—
Easily, easily.

Tomorrow the cream-clouds will be fouled.
The sky will be buckshot-full of paratroop swarms
With their money-talking guns,
Headlines carved across their foreheads,
Sophisticated, silent electrical equipment.
Heart-screws and fear-throwers.
The day after tomorrow
The clouds will curdle, the clouds will begin to burn—
Yes, we expected that, knew about that,
Overkill, overburn, multi-megacorpse,
Yeah, yeah, yeah we knew about that
Cry the white-hearted flies.

Channel One—
A fly scientist in an ivory helmet
Who always appears about to cry
Explains why the viewers have to die.

Channel Nine—
A fly statesman,
Hardly audible through the acid rain,
Explains why nothing can ever happen again.

e interpreter said 'he has to stand, cannot sit or lie.' he had to stand-because his

Oh we'll soon be finished with the creatures of the earth.
There's no future in elephants, milk or Asiatics.
We should be working out
How to inflict the maximum pain
On Martians and Venusians.

Sour sky.
The elephants are entering the shed.
Sour sky.
The flies have dropped a star called Wormwood
And turned the Pacific into an acid bath.
Sour sky.
Socrates said no harm could come to a good man,
But even Socrates
Couldn't turn the hemlock into a banana milk-shake
With one high-voltage charge
From his Greek-sky eyes.
Even Socrates, poor bugger.

They are rubbing their forelegs together,
Washing each others' holes with their stubbled tongues,
Watching us while they wash.
Then, like brown rain running backwards,
They hurtle upwards, vibrating with acid.
They patrol our ceilings, always looking downwards.
Pick up the phone, that's them buzzing.
The turd-born flies.

Peace is milk
And milk is simple
And milk is hard to make.
It takes clean grass, fed by clean earth, clean air, clean rain,
Takes a calm cow with all her stomachs working
And it takes milk to raise that cow.

body was no longer covered with a skin but with a crust like crackling which broke easil

The milk is not for the good elephant.
The milk is not for the bad elephant.
But the milk may be for the lucky elephant
Looming along until the end of the kingdom of the flies.

A family of people, trapped in Death Valley,
Drank from the radiator,
Laid out the hubcaps as bowls for the dew,
Buried each other up to the neck in sand
And waited for better times, which came
Just after they stopped hoping.*

So the sweet survival of the elephants demands
Vision, cunning, energy and possibly burial
Until, maybe, the good times roll for the first time
And a tidal wave of elephants,
A stampede of milk,
Tornadoes through the capitals of flydom,
Voices flow like milk,
And below the white, nourishing depths—
Bodies moving any way they want to move,
Eyes resting or dancing at will,.
Limbs and minds which follow, gladly,
The music of the milk.

So you drink my milk, I'll drink yours.
We'll melt together in the sun
Despite the high-explosive flies
Which hover, which hover,
Which hover, which hover,
Like a million plaguey Jehovahs.

*true story from Time Magazine

front of us a curious figure was standing, a little crouched, legs straddled, arms out-

Their prisons, their police, their armies, their laws,
Their camps where Dobermans pace the cadaver of a field,
Their flame factories and Black Death Factories,
The sourness of their sky—
Well that's the poisonous weather the elephants must
    lumber through,
Surviving, surviving,
Until the good times roll for the first time.

But it doesn't end
With an impregnable city carved out of the living light.
It doesn't end
In the plastic arms of an Everest-size Sophia Loren.
It doesn't end
When the world says a relieved farewell to the white man
As he goofs off to colonize the Milky Way.

It continues, it continues.
When all of the elephants push it goes slowly forward.
When they stop pushing it rolls backwards.
It continues, it continues.
Towards milk, towards acid.

The taste of milk has been forgotten.
Most elephants agree peace is impossible.
Choosing death instead, they are jerked towards death
Slowly by newspapers, nightmares or cancer,
More quickly by heroin or war.
And some, the tops of their skulls sliced off
By money-knives or the axes of guilt,
Bow their great heads and let their hurting brains
Slop in the lavatory to drown.

stretched from his sides. he had no eyes and his body, most of which was visible throug

There are prophets—grand-children of William Blake—*
Desperate elephants who drink a pint of diamonds.
Their eyes become scored with a thousand white trenches,
Their hide shines with a constellation
Of diamond-headed boils,
Each footstep leaves a pool of diamond dust.
And sure, they shine,
They become shouting stars,
Burning with light until they are changed by pain
Into diamonds for everyone.
And sure, they go down shining,
They shine themselves to death,
The diamond drinkers.

The world is falling to pieces
But some of the pieces taste good.

There are various ways of making peace,
Most of them too childish for English elephants.
Given time and love it's possible
To cultivate a peace-field large enough
For the playing of a child.
It's possible to prepare a meal
And give it with care and love
To someone who takes it with care and love.
These are beginnings, but it's late, late—
TV Dinner tonight.
It's possible to suck the taste of peace
From one blade of grass
Or recognise peace in a can of white paint,
But it's not enough.
In Nirvana there's only room for one at a time.

* Allen Ginsberg and many others

tatters of burnt rags, was covered with a hard black crust speckled with yellow pus. . . .

WELL, YOU COULD STOP KILLING PEOPLE FOR A START.

Let loose the elephants.
Let the fountains talk milk.
Free the grass, let it walk wherever it likes.
Let the passports and prisons burn, their
    smoke turning into milk.
Let the pot-smokers blossom into milk-coloured mental
    petals.
We all need to be breast-fed
And start again.

Tear the fly-woven lying suits
Off the backs of the white killers
And let their milky bodies
Make naked pilgrimage
To wash the sores of Africa and Asia
With milk, for milk is peace
And money tastes of guns,
Guns taste of acid.

*Make love well, generously, deeply.
There's nothing simpler in the savage world,
Making good love, making good good love.
There's nothing harder in the tender world,
Making good love, making good good love,
And most of the elephants, most of the time
Go starving for good love, not knowing what the pain is,
But it can be done and thank Blake it is done,
Making good love, making good good love.
In houses built of fly-turds, in fly-turd feasting mansions,
Fly-fear insurance offices even,
Fly-worshipping cathedrals even,
Even in murder offices just off the corridors of fly-power—
Making good love, making good good love.

* I use "make love" here and in "To You" because the phrase has the breadth to include not only sexual love-making but the creation of love in every possible way — the making of music, warmth to strangers etc.

the interpreter said 'he has to stand, cannot sit or lie.' he had to stand-because his

        Good lovers float,
        Happy to know they are becoming real.
        They float out and above the sourness, high on the seeds
           of peace.
        There are too few of them up there.
        Too little milk.
        Drink more milk.
        Breed more cows and elephants.
        Think more milk and follow your banana.
        We need evangelist, door-to-door lovers,
        Handing it out, laying it down,
        Spreading the elephant seed, delivering the revolutionary
           milk,
        Making good love, making good good love.
        United Nations teams of roving elephant milkmen
        Making good love, making good good love,
        Because peace is milk,
        Peace is milk
        And the skinny, thirsty earth, its face covered with flies,
        Screams like a baby.

body was no longer covered with a skin but with a crust like crackling which broke easily.

For Anyone, But Especially For:

ALISTAIR ANNE ALLEN ANDY ALBERT ANN ANTHONY ADRIAN ANSELM ARNOLD ANGUS ALEX ANNIKA ALAN ANNIE ANNA BEATRIX BRIONY BARBARA BILL BOB BRIAN BARRY CELIA CLARE CHRISTOPHER CLAIRE CLIVE CONNIE CLAUDE CLANCY DANNY DAVID DON DOROTHY DOUG DIDA DIXIE DICK DIBBY DIANE DUSTY ETAIN ELEANOR EDNA ETHEL ELIZABETH FIDEL FERGUS FRED FRANK FREDDIE FRAN GORDON GAYE GEOFFREY GARRY GEORGE HARRY HOPPY HELEN HUGH HATTIE HENRY HAMISH IRVING IRENE ISLA JOAN JOCK JAMES JIMMY JOHN JEAN JULIET JERRY JOHNNY JOE JANE JENNY JUDY JONATHAN JEREMY JIM JAN JEFF JAY KEN KATY KATHLEEN KARL KIKA LLEW LAWRENCE LESLEY LEON LIPPY LIZ LIBBY LAURIE LAURA MAUREEN MARK MARCIA MICHAEL MARGO MERRY MELOR MARIA-GLORIA MIKE MEGGIE MARTIN MARJORIE MARY MARIA MOIRA MAX MILES MARGARET MAL NICK NORMAN NATASHA NAT OCTAVIO OLIVIA OSCAR OWEN PATRICK PAUL PETER PENNY PAULINE PETE PEGGY PHILIP PABLO PAT REX ROSEMARY RUTH REGGIE ROGER ROSE ROLAND RED RUDI RON RICHARD RAM ROBIN ROBERT RUSTY SASHA SHIRLEY SUE SEAMUS SALLY SIAN SIMONE SEAN SHEILA STUART SPIKE SYDNEY TRIX TONY TOM THURLOW THABO TROY TILLY TREVOR URSULA WENDY WILLIE ZELIDE—AND MANY OTHERS WHO HAVE GIVEN LOVINGLY TO ME.

hundreds more since then...

By the same author

IF YOU SEE ME COMIN' (novel)
POEMS
Marat/Sade. (verse adaptation of Peter Weiss play. Calder and Boyars) The Magic Flute. (English version. Friends of Covent Garden). The Ledge. (Libretto. for Richard Rodney Bennett opera. Mills Music). Punch and Judas. (Puppet play written with Michael Kustow. CND). Poems. (Transatlantic Records EP). Poetry and Jazz (Argo Records LP). Fantasy Poets No. 24 (Fantasy Press).

Acknowledgments

Poems in this book have previously appeared in Challenge, East Village Other, Flourish, ICA Bulletin, Impact, International Times, Labour Monthly, Manchester Independent, New British Poetry, New Gambit, New Statesman, Peace News, The People's World, Poetry Review, Priapus, Resistance, Solidarity, Sunday Times, Topolski's Chronicle, Transatlantic Review, Tribune, Underdog, Underground and Wholly Communion, *but not The Beano.* They have been broadcast by BBC radio, Pacifica radio, BBC TV, ATV and STV. Several of them were used, set to Richard Peaslee's music, in the Royal Shakespeare Company's "US" and two of them were included in Peter Whitehead's film "Wholly Communion".

The quotation which runs along the top of each page is used by kind permission of Mr Rene Cutforth.

~~This second edition was Designed, Printed & Published by Cape Goliard Press Ltd, 102 Fairhazel Gardens, London N.W.6, 1969.~~

Printed in Great Britain

A 54-year-old deaf mute was found guilty today at West Ham of using insulting words. P.C. Charles Fillery said he heard the accused, no fixed address, shout "unintelligibly" at three women and a man in Barking Road, Plaistow. When he was remanded in custody for a week for a medical report, he was led away crying.

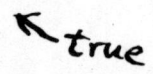

← true

This first annotated edition published by Writers + Readers Publishing Cooperative, 14 Talacre Road, London NW5 3PE